THAT'S WHAT
MAKES YOU
SPECIAL!

An Inspirational Activity Book
& Monthly Journal

Gilly Goodwin

'Because paper has more patience than people'

Anne Frank

CONTENTS

FORWARD

This is a part-activity book and part-journal, containing a guide to explore your thoughts, hopes, and dreams for the future – with inspiring quotes, pictures and shared reflections.

The journal is interspersed with pictures / photos and quotations – all carefully chosen to spark ideas and maybe a sense of wonder. A few tasks, comments and guidance are included, followed where necessary, by a page in which to fulfil those tasks.

The activities are intended to help you to reflect on the past, search through your thoughts and move on to motivate and inspire your future.

Some sections ask you to dip into your own memories and dreams and formulate some lists for yourself, followed by some further activities which will direct your thoughts towards planning for a positive future with some achievable goals. This does not, however, replace those long-term hopes and dreams which may seem impossible at the moment.

It is not meant to be a series of strict events and instructions but rather a more general and relaxed guide – approaching the topics in a more unusual and creative way and leaving room for you to write some thoughts down for your own benefit.

A few suggestions ...

This is meant to be completed over a period of time – so don't be afraid to work on some sections and then complete them later – after some thought processes have had a chance to evolve and grow.

Please ask yourself WHY I have picked particular pictures. What are they meant to depict? Do they hold a message of some kind?

I have to admit that I chose some because they made me smile and feel encouraged and I chose others because I thought 'wow'!

I make no apologies for all the dog pictures!

This is meant to be a 'special' book to keep for the future, so make the activities 'special' too.

Find a special pen to use – just for this activity journal.

Find a special place to write i.e. somewhere quiet
... An inspiring view of the garden
... In front of a favourite picture
... With a relaxing piece of music

ONE

'The future belongs to those who believe in the beauty of their dreams'

Eleanor Roosevelt

Section One

Aim ... to make you think more about your individuality
and to start writing!

Task One

Write your full name on the opposite page (in big letters) – then
see how many words you can make out of it. Pronouns,
abbreviations and plurals are all fine! Try to fill the page.

Task Two

When you have finished, look closely at the words. This may be
completely accidental – or you may have chosen subconsciously –
but do any of them apply to you or even how you are feeling? Do
some make you laugh, smile or even make you cringe?
Underline the ones you feel are positive.

Sharing

I have chosen just a few words I can make out of my name.
N.B. I have used my full first name and a middle name too. Some
underlined words have been chosen for obvious positivity!

<u>Good</u>	<u>Win</u>	<u>Wins</u>	Will	Wills	Yell
Sell	Selling	<u>Willing</u>	Wine	Swine	
Leylines	Swill	Wood	Silly	Wing	Swing
Nailing	Winding	<u>Dealing</u>	<u>Yes!</u>	Dwelling	

Section One – Worksheet

Full Name: _____

Words ... ...

TWO

'But I know, somehow, that only when it is dark enough - can you see the stars'

Martin Luther King Jr.

Section Two

Aim ... to discover what makes you special
within the whole universe.

Task One

Try to make a list of ten things that make you 'special' ......

Try to pick some items, people or characteristics that make you unique and therefore only apply to you

Task Two

Choose a dark but clear evening to look up at the sky at night and try to really visualise the immense size of the universe. While you do so – think of each one of the items which make you 'special' in this unfathomable space. (Get away from streetlights if you can)!

If you have ever done this before – you will know why I have set this task.

Sharing

1) You will need to think about this carefully – you may want to include general items but also be more specific about people, relationships, physical characteristics, talents etc. Take your time over this one ... rejoice in eccentricities and the unusual.

2) Make yourself comfortable so that you can really look intently at the sky and stars. Those stars which took billions of years just for the light to reach YOU at that moment in time!

I am sometimes overwhelmed at the size of our universe and find it difficult to comprehend. The word 'awesome' does not do it justice – and yet we are here on a unique beautiful blue planet which has overcome all the odds.

Section Two - Worksheet

1

2

3

4

5

6

7

8

9

10

THREE

Nothing is impossible ...
The word itself says ...
I'm possible!
Audrey Hepburn

If you think you are too small to make a difference ...
try sleeping with a mosquito
The Dalai Lama

Be happy ...
It drives people crazy!
Unknown

Section Three

Aim ... to continue to explore and discover more about yourself, your character, your likes and dislikes.

Task One

Choose 10 things (or programmes or people etc.) that make you actually laugh out loud. That laugh may be an enormous roar of laughter or may be more of a chuckle!

Task Two

Try to work out what it actually is that has caused such a response from you. Is it (or are they) crude ... coarse ... witty ... sarcastic ... quick-witted ... showy ... well-rehearsed etc?

Add your own comments alongside.

Sharing

There are only a few comedians who actually make me laugh out loud. I personally prefer TV programmes or books and can usually be heard sniggering over some witty comments.

I appreciate quickness and timing ... also something that might have taken a long time to rehearse such as some of the clever routines by the Two Ronnies. But I am showing my age here and you will have different reasons for actually laughing out loud.

You might want to complete this section in smaller stages rather than all at once.

Section Three – Worksheet

1

2

3

4

5

6

7

8

9

10

FOUR

*You must move on – just let it go –
don't dwell on the past …
Forgive yourself and others,
then move forward.
Enjoy life and benefit from it.*

Gilly Goodwin

Section Four

Aims ... to identify the experiences which stir your emotions
... to attempt to deal with them in a positive way.

Task One

Now do the same as section three, but with things that make you cry. Yes – these might be tears of unhappiness – but they might be tears of appreciation, respect and sadness for others or for animals or maybe tears of regret - for things that have happened in the past that cannot be put right.

Task Two

Maybe you like just having a cry over a good film or perhaps you can help resolve some of these by doing your share for charities etc. but some of these will probably be personal. Is there anything **you** can do to make amends or are these the things that just need to be put away? Not forgotten ... but if we can't make them right, then should we put them down to experience and learn from them?

Try to write a few comments for yourself on the table provided.

Sharing

I can cry over anything ... animal cruelty, films (particularly if the music resonates with what is happening on screen), sad stories on the news etc. But I also regret some decisions I have made in the past.

If your tears were shed over the past, then by all means try to make amends – but if this is difficult or impossible – then you must move on. These regrets are the things that define you as a person and we all learn from our mistakes!

Do you ever laugh so much that you cry tears of joy? Can you link the last two sections in any way?

And don't forget ....

'For millions of years, mankind lived just like the animals.
Then something happened which unleashed the power of
our imagination.
We learned to talk and we learned to listen.
Speech has allowed the communication of ideas, enabling
human beings to work together to build the impossible.
Mankind's greatest achievements have come about by talking
... ... and its greatest failures by not talking'

Stephen Hawking

Section Four – Worksheet

1

2

3

4

5

6

7

8

9

10

FIVE

And then a hero comes along
With the strength to carry on
And you cast your fears aside
And you know you can survive
When you feel like hope is gone
Look inside you and be strong
And you'll finally see the truth
That a hero lies in you

Mariah Carey

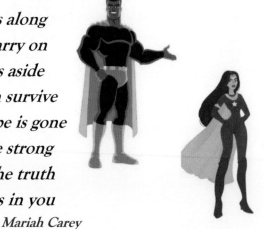

Section Five

Aim ... Two sections to identify and explore the hero in others ... and then in yourself.

Task One

Write down 10 **celebrities** who – for you – are heroes. They can be from sport / TV / Radio / Politics / Books / Films / Music etc. etc. You choose ... they are **your** heroes.

Task Two

Now try to work out **why** they have your respect and interest. Is it their ability or talent? Maybe it is their humour or their general personality traits. Maybe it is just because they are popular and famous and you admire them for that?

Add some comments to your list.

Sharing

Over the years – I have tried to formulate a hero list on a number of occasions. Something happens so that they are brought to my notice – and I think *'that would be a good one to add to my hero list'* ... but I never get to write them down and then I forget.

You can start your own hero list at the back of this journal – keep adding to it and look back over it over the years – to see if your opinions have changed or whether they still mean as much to you as when you initially chose them.

Section Five – Worksheet

1

2

3

4

5

6

7

8

9

10

SIX

'A friend in need is a friend indeed"

Unknown

SECTION SIX

Aim ... to identify and explore those everyday heroes you know
and who are closer to home.

Task One

Now pick 10 heroes you know personally. They may be relatives /
friends / people who have stood by you in times of crisis / teachers
or tutors / professionals who may have had contact with you / just
general people you admire etc. etc.

Task Two

Perhaps the more difficult task – this may take a longer period
of reflection.

Just WHY do these people mean so much to you? Are they good
listeners? Do they put others before themselves? Do they go out of
their way to help or to impart their own knowledge and skills to
others?

Try to add some comments to your list.

Sharing

I am a firm believer in the saying at the start of the section – *'a
friend in need is a friend indeed.'* In other words – someone who is in
need of a friend, really values 'friendship' itself and would make an
excellent companion.

Does your list contain someone who fills this criterion?

If so – then now comes an important point on which to reflect ...
Does this person need your support as much as you need theirs?
Are you a good listener? Can you put other people's problems before
your own in order to return the compliment and help the friendship
work both ways?

Section Six – Worksheet

1

2

3

4

5

6

7

8

9

10

SEVEN

When one door of happiness closes, another opens; but often we look so long at the closed door that we do not see the one which has been opened for us.

Helen Keller

SECTION SEVEN

Aim – to explore the idea of having a dream career or future.

Task One

Go on the internet to look up a list of careers. Pick 10 that you think you would like to pursue in the future. Do these careers have any similarities? i.e. caring / nursing / medicine / welfare / animals etc. (N.B. This is only one example of possible similarities and will obviously depend on the careers you have chosen).

You may want to do this in retrospect if you are tackling this journal as an older and more experienced person.

Task Two

Think carefully about your choice. Is there an obvious reason for each of the careers you have chosen? Do any of them have a connection with your likes / dislikes / choice of heroes etc.

Do they require particular qualifications or talents?

If you haven't listed these in order of preference – please indicate your own order on the chart.

Sharing

This topic is not meant to offer any careers advice - so this section can either be explored in more detail (maybe with advice from some professionals) or can be left and treated as an aim or a possible objective for the future. It *is* meant to help you to continue exploring your dreams.

Section Seven - Worksheet

1

2

3

4

5

6

7

8

9

10

EIGHT

In your own mind ... using your own imagination... you can travel anywhere!

Gilly Goodwin

SECTION EIGHT

Aim ... To explore the type of world that exists
in your own heart and mind.

Task One

Make a list of the 10 ultimate places in the world that you would like to visit. These may be for the purpose of a holiday – or just because of a fascination with the landmark or history of the place.

Task Two

Look carefully at your list; maybe do some extra research. Is there any type of connection between the places you have chosen?

Do they have certain characteristics i.e. landscapes – historical significance – sporting venues - buildings – animal habitats etc.

Add a few comments and thoughts to your list.

Sharing

There are many places I would like to visit, so this would take me a long time to work out what my favourite 10 would include.

They would however, include places of great scenic beauty, some animal habitats and some famous historical landmarks.

My favourite ...

Maybe somewhere I could swim with dolphins :-)

Gilly Goodwin

Section Eight - Worksheet

1

2

3

4

5

6

7

8

9

10

NINE

'Every child is an artist; the problem is staying an artist when you grow up'

Pablo Picasso

'A diamond is merely a lump of coal that did well under pressure'

Unknown

'Music expresses that which cannot be put into words and that which cannot remain silent'

Victor Hugo

SECTION NINE

Aim ... To explore and utilise your gifts and talents

Task One

Try to make a list of 10 talents or abilities you possess. These may be very specific e.g. Piano grade 5 – or more general as in being a good friend or a good listener.

Task Two

Look carefully at your list. Are there some talents you would like to add to the list? Can you group some talents together i.e. sport/ music/ drama/ co-ordination/ social talents/ academic etc.

Add some extra comments to your list.

Sharing

This section also connects closely with the 'Section Ten' activities on hobbies so don't worry if your thoughts overlap.

If you feel unable to fill in all 10 spaces – then try to do some research online to give you more ideas.

This may bring up the age-old discussion as to what is a talent, a gift or a skill. What do you think?

Are your talents transferable to others – i.e. could you teach them or pass on your knowledge and skills to others in the future?

Could your talents be used to help your friends? This can be a good way to start talking to them more personally and mindfully.

Section Nine - Worksheet

1

2

3

4

5

6

7

8

9

10

TEN

'Happy is the man who can make a living by his hobby'

George Bernard Shaw

'When I was about eight, I decided that the most wonderful thing, next to a human being, was a book'

Margaret Walker

'One day, you will be old enough to start reading fairytales again'

C.S. Lewis

SECTION TEN

Aim ... To help you to reinforce, strengthen and develop all your hobbies and interests.

Task One

Try to list 10 of your hobbies and interests on the next page. If you run out of ideas – list some you would wish to pursue in the future. (Maybe you could avoid any that coincide with your 'talents' mentioned in the last section).

Task Two

Look carefully at your list. Can you group some of them together? Do you need to add to your list? How good are you at each hobby and could they be added to your talent list?

Add some comments to your list and rank them in order of importance to you and then rank them again based on your ability level for each hobby.

Sharing

Are your hobbies general activities that can be pursued anytime e.g. reading? Or do they require certain pieces of equipment? Or maybe they are only available at specific times of the day e.g. sport/ music etc.

Just how good are you at these hobbies? Can any of these be developed further for work purposes?

More importantly – are you someone who does not have many hobbies or interests? How many of your hobbies involve interaction or conversation with others? Do you need to introduce yourself to some new hobbies which are more social and will help you to meet other people with similar interests?

Section Ten - Worksheet

1

2

3

4

5

6

7

8

9

10

BE CREATIVE

'Challenge yourself creatively and make your dreams a reality'

Anonymous

'Creativity is a wild mind and a disciplined eye'

Dorothy Parker

'Creative people are curious, flexible, persistent, and independent, with a tremendous spirit of adventure and a love of play'

Henri Matisse

Be Creative - Continued

Aim ... to design your own autobiographical book cover

Task One

Read back through your earlier choices and lists and try to decide what you have learnt about yourself. If you wrote an autobiography about your life so far – what title would you give it? Add that title to the template on the following page.

Task Two

Now decide what colours, patterns and images you would use to enhance your book cover. Add these to the template.

Sharing

This is not intended to be a dry factual title and theme for the book. BE CREATIVE! All things are possible.

Explore imaginative, inspiring words and choose the best title that is personal to you and reveals something of yourself.

Do the same with any images and colours you may use on your book cover.

N.B. Don't settle for something if you don't feel it is quite right. Wait and take your time.

Would you use your own name – or a pen-name?

Do you need a sub-title which can reveal more information about yourself?

Are your images/pictures influenced by your earlier lists?

Have you used any words and ideas from those lists?

Use the next few sections to explore your creativity.

BOOK COVER WORKSHEET

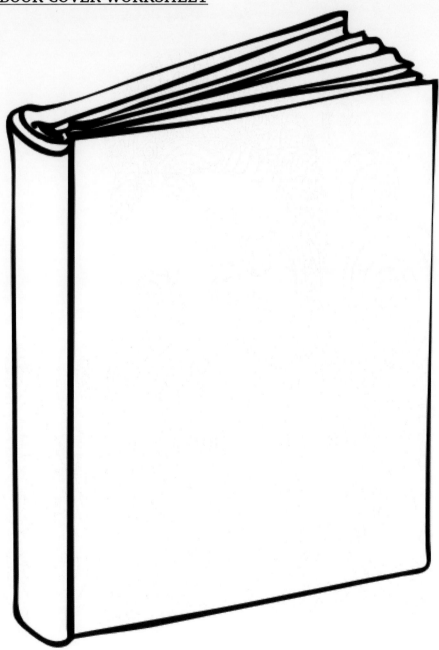

HOROSCOPE

'The greatest adventure is what lies ahead
Today and tomorrow are yet to be said
The chances, the changes
                        are all yours to make
The mould of your life
                        is in your hands to break'

J.R.R. Tolkien

'Just because the past didn't turn out
like you wanted, doesn't mean your future
can't be better than you imagined'

Anonymous

'The best way to predict the future is to create it'

Abraham Lincoln

Horoscope - Continued

Aim ... to compose your own horoscope based on your hopes and dreams for the future.

Task One
Research a few horoscopes over the next few days – trying to read some from different astrologers and from different star signs - not just your own.

Task Two
Compose your own horoscope being as creative as you can – write it out on the next page. Make sure you think about your future without making it too unrealistic.
Make it achievable with some good luck and a little effort.

Sharing
You will find that most horoscopes are written in very general terms, as they have to be – in order to fulfil their purpose.
I would like you to create your horoscope with more personal aims and individual ideas.

Read back over the earlier sections of the workbook and decide which parts really resonate with you and have caused the biggest reaction from you as you have worked through the pages.

I would try to imagine where you would like to be in a few years' time – perhaps don't aim too far in the future for this – you can always update it or write another that reaches further into your dreams.

HOROSCOPE

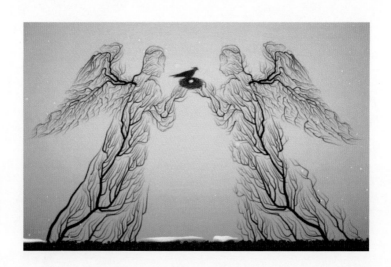

TREE OF LIFE

'Walk tall as the trees; live strong as the mountains;
Be gentle as the spring winds;
Keep the warmth of the summer sun in your heart
And the Great Spirit will always be with you'

Native American proverb

'Even if I knew that tomorrow the world would go to
pieces, I would still plant my apple tree'

Martin Luther

'Do not be afraid to go out on a limb...
That's where the fruit is'

Anonymous

49

TREE OF LIFE – Continued

Aim ... To design your own 'Tree of Life'

Task One

Draw a few leaves on the branches of the tree design on the next page. Make sure they are large enough to add a word or short phrase inside them.

Decide what words should be added to those leaves which would make up your own Tree of Life – see the suggestions below.

Add them to the design.

Task Two

I have particularly picked a design that still retains some roots.

What are the 'roots' of your own tree? Can you add some words near the roots which form the foundations of your own life?

Add some colour to the design to make it more 'special'.

Sharing

Some suggestions ...

Add people/ items/ thoughts/ places etc. which form the basis of your life and day to day actions.

e.g. Family/ home (house)/ town/ friends/ school life or work life/ health/ animals (pets)/ special hobbies / sports/ beliefs or ethics/ political viewpoints/ leisure time activities etc.

Maybe you even have to mention important items you own e.g. personal equipment/ jewellery/ nostalgic items (memories)/ musical instruments/ car or bike/ photos/ favourite belongings etc.

N.B. These are only suggestions to start your thinking processes. You should be choosing items or people etc. that are necessary to your continued well-being and your successful future life.

So – bring your tree to life!

Tree of Life

MEDITATE

'When we recognize our place in an immensity of
light years and in the passage of ages ...
When we grasp the intricacy, beauty and
subtlety of life, then that soaring feeling,
that sense of elation and humility combined ...
is surely spiritual.'

Carl Sagan

'The moment you wake up each morning, all your wishes
and hopes for the day rush at you like wild animals,
and the first job each morning consists of
shoving it all back; in listening to that other voice,
taking that other point of view, letting that other,
larger, stronger, quieter life come flowing in.'

C. S. Lewis

Meditate - Continued

Aims ... To set aside a time each day that is just for you
... To enable you to calm your thoughts and
let the stresses of the day fade into insignificance.
... To explore your spirituality

Task One

Find a special place that makes you feel confident, comfortable and is peaceful and stress free.

Spend at least 30-60 minutes breathing slowly and deeply. Find a relaxed position and depending on your mood - play some music which makes you feel calm and relaxed ... or happy and vibrant.

Don't do anything else. Don't remember the day or worry about the future – just live for the moment!

Task Two

N.B. This is an 'occasional' task, for when you might need it.

There is always a place for tears. Everyone should be able to feel that, on occasion, they can 'let it all out' and have a good cry. It is not a sign of weakness – but a sign that you are aware of your own emotions and it is important that you don't tie yourself into knots trying not to let it show.

Use a piece of music (the suggestions on the next page are just *suggestions* – you will have your own ideas), just sit quietly and if the tears flow don't stop them – but don't force them either – go with the flow!

It is a good idea to share this task with a trusted friend and to talk afterwards.

Sharing

A definition of the word *'spiritual'* includes ... relating to the spirit or soul, as distinguished from the physical nature.

Other related words and phrases include ... inner being; thoughts rather than physical actions; finding yourself; inner strength; seeking the 'divine' within yourself; celestial; intangible; sacred.

I hope this helps you to reach into your own spirituality while meditating.

Sometimes, I just want to sit still - in silence - or with a piece of music playing in the background and think of nothing ... to just sit there, letting all the pressures of the day fade away.

I make no apologies for my choice of music suggestions on the next page – they suit me – but therefore may not suit you. They are only suggestions as to the 'type' of piece you might want to use.

There is a real mixture here from Light 'pop' – Classical – Film Music – organ pieces etc.

Choose your own pieces if you prefer, or just meditate in silence.

If I can convert anyone into loving my favourite piece ...

good!

Upbeat/ Lively ... Not for meditation – but to help change your mood?

Hey Soul Sister (Train)

Walking on Sunshine (Katrina and the Waves)

Billie Jean (Michael Jackson)

Rhythm of Life (Sweet Charity)

Mr. Blue Sky (ELO)

La Calinda (Delius) (London Philharmonic version) ... My favourite piece!

Wedding Day at Troldhaugen (Grieg)

Toccata (Widor)

Palladio (Karl Jenkins)

Candide Overture (Bernstein)

Inspirational/ Thoughtful/ Emotional ... (Meditation?)

You've got a Friend (James Taylor)

We've Only Just Begun (Carpenters)

A Thousand Years (Christina Perry)

Just the Way You Are (Billy Joel)

You Are Not Alone (Michael Jackson)

If it's Magic (Stevie Wonder)

Albatross (Fleetwood Mac)

When You Believe (Hans Zimmer/ Whitney Houston)

I'm Not in Love (10CC)

Windmills of your Mind (Noel Harrison)

Schindler's List (John Williams)

Empire of the Sun (John Williams)

Time (Hans Zimmer)

Adagio for strings (Samuel Barber)

Benedictus (Karl Jenkins)

Pie Jesu (Faure and/or Karl Jenkins)

Rhosymedre (Vaughan-Williams)

Cello Concerto (Elgar)

Violin Concerto (Bruch)

Hymn of the Cherubim (Tchaikovsky))

TIMELINE

'It does not matter how slowly you go as long as you do not stop'

Confucius

'There is nothing like a dream to create the future'

Victor Hugo

'The bad news is time flies. The good news is you're the pilot.'

Anonymous

Timeline – Continued

Aim ... To recap and sum-up your ideas and your input into this journal/workbook
... To try to create your own timeline for the future

Task One

Read back – flick through – cross out - add comments – make new entries – reflect – explore – discover etc.

Read back through the journal and identify how it has made you feel and what effects it has had on your recent thoughts.

Task Two

Try to create your own timeline on the next page. Include your hopes and dreams yes – but be sensible too.

You decide on the timescale – i.e. months – years – decades?

Sharing

When I have used this exercise in the past – students have always gone out of their way to make this a special page. They have added colours, small diagrams and have used different fonts to create almost a poster of their future as they see it.

You decide on the timescale to suit you. Do you need to do a detailed plan of the next year? Is it an important year – a new stage in your life? Or do you need to spread it out and plan in more general terms for a larger number of years or even decades?

Remember – these are only ideas – something to aim for – something to explore in the future. It does not have to be set in stone and unworkable. It will obviously be subject to change and development, as time forges ever onwards.

You may wish to create your own mind-map instead of a timeline.

TIMELINE

DESIDERATA

In order to clarify why you have been set certain tasks in the journal and also to summarise the guidance and advice given ...

... 'Desiderata' seems to do most of it for me – so I have included it on the next page.

Desiderata in Latin means – 'things desired'.

Desiderata is a poem for a way of life, written in 1927 by the American lawyer and writer Max Ehrmann (1872 – 1945).
It was largely unknown in the author's lifetime, but its widespread use in 1960's and 1970's brought it to the attention of the world.

DESIDERATA

Go placidly amid the noise and the haste, and remember what peace there may be in silence.

As far as possible, without surrender, be on good terms with all persons. Speak your truth quietly and clearly; and listen to others, even to the dull and the ignorant; for they too have their story.

Avoid loud and aggressive persons; they are vexatious to the spirit. If you compare yourself with others, you may become vain or bitter, for always there will be greater and lesser persons than yourself.

Enjoy your achievements as well as your plans. Keep interested in your own career, however humble; it is a real possession in the changing fortunes of time. Exercise caution in your business affairs, for the world is full of trickery. But let this not blind you to what virtue there is; many persons strive for high ideals and everywhere life is full of heroism.

Be yourself. Especially do not feign affection. Neither be cynical about love, for in the face of all aridity and disenchantment, it is as perennial as the grass.

Take kindly the counsel of the years, gracefully surrendering the things of youth. Nurture strength of spirit to shield you in sudden misfortune. But do not distress yourself with dark imaginings. Many fears are born of fatigue and loneliness.

Beyond a wholesome discipline, be gentle with yourself. You are a child of the universe no less than the trees and the stars; you have a right to be here. And whether or not it is clear to you, no doubt the universe is unfolding as it should.

Therefore be at peace with God, whatever you conceive Him to be. And whatever your labours and aspirations, in the noisy confusion of life, keep peace in your soul.

With all its sham, drudgery, and broken dreams, it is still a beautiful world.

Be cheerful. Strive to be happy.

MONTHLY JOURNAL

The second half of the workbook contains a journal and some extra pages to start your own Bucket and Hero Lists.

This will obviously be 'a work in progress' and it is up to you to continue with it as you wish or to leave it and reflect on it for a while. You can always return to it at a later date.

The journal allows 2 pages per month – with some extra pages for additional notes at the end. You can start in whichever month you prefer. It is 'work in progress' and is therefore not restricted to a particular year.

My suggestions would be to include information about anything that has been triggered from the earlier sections – or maybe about the achievements and goals you have included on your timeline.
Perhaps write about the month in retrospect – as you move into a new month?

Good luck

Be careful. Strive to be happy!

JANUARY

... continued

_____

_____

_____

_____

_____

_____

_____

_____

_____

_____

_____

_____

_____

_____

_____

_____

_____

_____

_____

_____

FEBRUARY

... continued

_____

_____

_____

_____

_____

_____

_____

_____

_____

_____

_____

_____

_____

_____

_____

_____

_____

_____

_____

_____

MARCH

... continued

_____

_____

_____

_____

_____

_____

_____

_____

_____

_____

_____

_____

_____

_____

_____

_____

_____

_____

_____

_____

APRIL

... continued

_____

_____

_____

_____

_____

_____

_____

_____

_____

_____

_____

_____

_____

_____

_____

_____

_____

_____

_____

MAY

... continued

_____

_____

_____

_____

_____

_____

_____

_____

_____

_____

_____

_____

_____

_____

_____

_____

_____

_____

_____

_____

JUNE

... *continued*

_____

_____

_____

_____

_____

_____

_____

_____

_____

_____

_____

_____

_____

_____

_____

_____

_____

_____

JULY

... continued

_____

_____

_____

_____

_____

_____

_____

_____

_____

_____

_____

_____

_____

_____

_____

_____

_____

_____

_____

_____

AUGUST

... continued

_____

_____

_____

_____

_____

_____

_____

_____

_____

_____

_____

_____

_____

_____

_____

_____

_____

_____

_____

SEPTEMBER

... continued

OCTOBER

... *continued*

_____

_____

_____

_____

_____

_____

_____

_____

_____

_____

_____

_____

_____

_____

_____

_____

_____

_____

NOVEMBER

... continued

_____

_____

_____

_____

_____

_____

_____

_____

_____

_____

_____

_____

_____

_____

_____

_____

_____

_____

_____

DECEMBER

... continued

_____

_____

_____

_____

_____

_____

_____

_____

_____

_____

_____

_____

_____

_____

_____

_____

_____

_____

ADDITIONAL NOTES

ADDITIONAL NOTES

HERO LISTS

BUCKET LIST

1	
2	
3	
4	
5	
6	
7	
8	
9	
10	
11	
12	
13	
14	
15	
16	
17	
18	

19
20
21
22
23
24
25
26
27
28
29
30
31
32
33
34
35
36
37
38

39	
40	
41	
42	
43	
44	
45	
46	
47	
48	
49	
50	

THOUGHTS?

ABOUT THE AUTHOR

Written and devised by Gilly Goodwin ... a highly experienced secondary school (11-18) teacher/practitioner for more than 20 years ... a tutor and co-ordinator on both the 'Gifted and Talented' and 'Aim Higher' programmes ... also helped to research the introduction of a Gifted and Talented programme in parts of the North West and North Wales.

Gilly Goodwin is also a music teacher, author and composer. She has written a number of children's stories (usually involving some kind of message of well-being or individuality) including **Pimple's Christmas** – (subtitled 'That's What Makes You Special') – **Pimple and the Snowman** (subtitled 'My Mum Says ...') and **The Fella in the Cellar** – as well as a middle-grade novel **Uriel ... A Whisper of Wings;** the first book of a trilogy intended for readers aged approx. 9-14 ... *and for any adults who have not completely given up their childhood!*

She lives with her husband in Southport (UK) and has two grown-up children. She loves all animals – particularly dogs and has recently owned two springer spaniels – Holly and Jazzy

As a Composer (using the name Gilly Goldsmith), Gilly has published the first volume of a book of new and original Carols -intended for various choral ensembles from SSA through to SATB.

Printed in Great Britain
by Amazon